SPIRIT-TAUGHT WORDS

Deborah Mebude

All scripture quotations, unless otherwise indicated, are taken from the New International Version®.

THE HOLY BIBLE, NEW INTERNATIONAL VERSION®, NIV® Copyright © 1973, 1978, 1984, 2011 by Biblica, Inc.® Used by permission. All rights reserved worldwide.

Scripture taken from the New King James Version®. Copyright © 1982 by Thomas Nelson. Used by permission. All rights reserved.

The ESV® Bible (The Holy Bible, English Standard Version®) copyright © 2001 by Crossway, a publishing ministry of Good News Publishers. ESV® Text Edition: 2011. The ESV® text has been reproduced in cooperation with and by permission of Good News Publishers. Unauthorized reproduction of this publication is prohibited. All rights reserved.

Scripture taken from *The Message*. Copyright © 1993, 1994, 1995, 1996, 2000, 2001, 2002. Used by permission of NavPress Publishing Group.

Scripture quotations marked (NLT) are taken from the Holy Bible, New Living Translation, copyright © 1996, 2004, 2007 by Tyndale House Foundation. Used by permission of Tyndale House Publishers, Inc., Carol Stream, Illinois 60188. All rights reserved.

Copyright © 2015 Deborah Mebude

All rights reserved. No part of this book may be reproduced in any form without explicit permission from the author.

ISBN-13: 978-1515381372

ISBN-10: 1515381374

*To the encouragers, the dreamers, the doubters, and the believers. To all those I'm blessed to call family and friends. To anyone who's ever offered a hand; a prayer; an ear to listen. This is my heart.
This is for you.*

"And I pray that you, being rooted and established in love, may have power, together with all the Lord's holy people, to grasp how wide and long and high and deep is the love of Christ, and to know this love that surpasses knowledge—that you may be filled to the measure of all the fullness of God." Ephesians 3:17-19

FORWARD

Dear beloved,

You are precious. You are valuable. You are worthy of love and you are cared for.

I preface this book with these admissions because it's essential you understand them, and if you don't already, my prayer is that once you're done here you will.

I'm here to share with you pieces of my heart and mind through poetry. My prayer is that you'd come to see the beauty of a life lived knowing the reality of a good God who is ever present and oh so delighted by you.

We could all use encouragement.

So here it is, my attempt to encourage you with the little I know about love, grace, freedom and faith; that you'd understand His love, experience His grace, discover His freedom, and come to faith.

"My message and my preaching were not with wise and persuasive words, but with a demonstration of the Spirit's power, so that your faith might not rest on human wisdom, but on God's power."
1 Corinthians 2:4-5

Table of Contents

LOVE	11
GRACE	43
FREEDOM	71
FAITH	103

"This is what we speak, not in words taught us by human wisdom but in words taught by the spirit, explaining Spiritual realities with Spirit-taught words."

1 Corinthians 2:13

LOVE

I think we all love the idea of love.

We're supposed to. We were designed to desire it and created to give it. But where do we begin in our broken, damaged world to make sense of what love is?

———————————————

"And over all these virtues put on love, which binds them all together in perfect unity." Colossians 3:14

Love

    This poem is about looking for love in all the wrong places and coming up short. It's about failing to accept the true love that is offered in Christ Jesus. It's about the soul craving in each one of our hearts to feel accepted as we are. It's about realizing that the unconditional, *agape* love that we've always longed for is not only within our grasp, but is overflowing, never ending, and greater than our wildest dreams. It's about learning to simply receive, not strain, or beg but understand that love is ours to have and ours to pass on. I hope the surpassing, infinitely intimate love of God becomes so, so real to you.

We need to learn to accept love.
Not the everyday generic stuff.
But.
The love that we crave.
That which we most thoroughly desire—the love of a father.
All other loves are derivative, secondary, less than.

We need the love that transcends all, that is before all, the love that feeds our innermost needs. The love that penetrates intimately.
We need that love.
God's love.
Our attempts to learn to love ourselves fail, have failed and always will because in our brokenness we are incapable of looking within and seeing even a glimpse of the beauty we've been formed in.
We barely see God.
How could we see the image we've been made in?
We can't find love from within, it must come from without.
From a God that is without conditions, without criteria, without a list of things we need to live up to, do well, or be good at.
A love without expectations. Without complications.
A love that loves because for it love is as natural as breathing
A love that loves because for it to love is to be.
See,
God IS love.

My broken attempts to love fall short because I am incapable.
My God is able.
My God is love.
And He wants me to accept the love He's been lavishing on me since day one.
A love that loves simply.
No complications.
A love that's ours for the taking.

"...Everyone who loves has been born of God and knows God. Whoever does not love does not know God, because God is love. This is how God showed his love among us: He sent his one and only Son into the world that we might live through him. This is love: not that we loved God, but that he loved us and sent his Son as an atoning sacrifice for our sins." 1 John 4:7-10

God is love. This is a statement with grave implications. To use the word "is" is to say that He exists as the physical embodiment, the literal characteristic of love. I don't know if there's anything that our souls crave more than love, if there's a single longing with greater magnitude than that to be adored, sought after, appreciated, and wanted. If God is love, then He is what our hearts desire more than anything, He must be the singular thing that fills the voids we are so apt to ignore, gloss over and pretend don't exist. If He's love, and we know love to be good, then He must not only be good, but the actual source of goodness and that from which goodness springs. The Bible says that those that don't know God don't know love, but those that know love know God. You may not think you've ever had a real encounter with God before, you may even doubt if He exists at all, but I assure you that if you've felt genuine love in any capacity, you've come in contact with God. The thing is though, and this is what is so outrageous, is that so much of the love that we've encountered is only a small picture of the full thing that exists in God Himself. The manifest presence of God is so much richer than the glimpses we've seen. The good news, nay, the greatest news in the universe, is that that love is available to each one of us. More than that, we don't have to fight or beg for it or even do anything to earn it. It's ours to have forever, it's our inheritance as children made in the image of God. All that's required is that you accept it. All you need to do is say yes to the God that is love itself.

Addendum: love

This was written not long after my first poem on the subject. As an addendum, I felt I had more to express concerning what exactly love is.

Love, relationship, friendship, all of it—is messy, there's no denying it. But the love of God in particular, a love that would slaughter and sacrifice its beloved for our sake, is gruesome.

I wanted to convey the multiple dimensions of a love that is so unconditional, so ferocious, so pure, and so good. I wanted to communicate the fact that love is in its very nature sacrificial and rough around the edges and that in that truth lies a deeper, fuller beauty that each of us need grab hold of. See God loved us to the point of death. His love is so real that it gave everything that it is. God doesn't hold back in any way when it comes to expressing His vast affection for us, and at the same time, desires that we'd do the same. That each of us would love with every single piece of us, giving Him our highest honour, adoration, praise, and devotion.

Love is messy.
Horribly,
Terribly,
Raw.
It wants the deepest parts of us
Beckons us to unearth the scars we've buried
The hurts that we've carried
Long forgotten
Insecurity,
Doubt,
Fear.
Ferocious
In its pursuit
Unrelenting
Deep dark wounds
Healed.
I've barely known love
At least in the traditional sense
But I've experienced love
I've experienced God
The author
Who authored the greatest story of love ever penned
Authorized the ascent

Divinity sent
A saviour marred
Scarlet.
Torn,
Martyred,
Scarred,
Red.
Raw
Terribly,
Horribly,
Messy.
God's love
Unrelenting;
Beckons us to die;
Welcomes us to life.

"Who, being in very nature God,
  did not consider equality with God something to be
 used to his own advantage;
 rather, he made himself nothing
  by taking the very nature of a servant,
  being made in human likeness.
 And being found in appearance as a man,

> he humbled himself
> by becoming obedient to death—
> > even death on a cross!"
> Philippians 2:5-8

"For God so loved the world that he gave his one and only Son, that whoever believes in him shall not perish but have eternal life." John 3:16

Love is sacrifice. It's in its very nature. Love compels the loving party to act on behalf of the object of love and sometimes this means taking drastic action or going to extreme measures to communicate said love. We've established that God is love; the implications of this truth are that it is in His very nature to give of Himself in a sacrificial, dramatic way. It's easy to see that humans are flawed. Turn on any news station for even a few moments and you will see that we are deeply broken and so in need of a saviour. "What causes fights and quarrels among you? Don't they come from your desires that battle within you? You desire but do not have, so you kill. You covet but you cannot get what you want, so you quarrel and fight" (James 4:1-2). We as humans exist in a perpetual state of destruction, our innate, default mode that of tearing down and harming. We fail to properly treat the people and environment around us. We lust and we abuse, we exploit, and we kill. Despite our tragic state, God chooses to love us. He does this because it's His nature and essence. He is love so that's what He does; in His pure, perfect state He looks down at a fallen humanity and does not leave us alone in our sorry condition, rather He intervenes and chooses to redeem. A verse that most with exposure to the Christian faith are familiar with is John 3:16. It says that God loved the world so much that He gave His only son. He did this, sacrificed His son Jesus on the cross, to bring us back into right relationship with Himself. Because He loves us, because He wants to see us know and experience who He is, He gave the thing most dear to Himself. This wasn't a small, insignificant sacrifice, this was one that would have broken His heart entirely. Death on a cross is a slow, excruciating one, and going through the physical, emotional, and spiritual anguish of that sacrifice was the ultimate display of affection. Love is beautiful, but so much of its beauty lies in its inhibited showmanship, the fact that it will literally give to the point of death. This is the kind of love that God offers, it's the kind He invites us into; it's messy, it's raw, it's incredible.

April Ninth Twenty Fourteen

I wrote this poem on a plane. I was tens of thousands of feet in the air and my mind wandered to thoughts of a God who descended from Heaven to meet with me. A great God. One that loved me enough to tuck His divinity in His back pocket and become sin in my place. And yet—I forsake Him.

In fact, I betray Him every single day and yet He still lavishes His amazing grace. It doesn't make a lot of sense. But His love is the kind that tends to be senseless, tends to love in a way that's pretty endless and that's something I love. And so I hope that I can live a life of gratitude to Him, giving back everything I've been given in offering, understanding that it was His in the first place. That every good and perfect gift was His to begin with and that a life spent in His presence, and for His purposes, is the best life lived.

Because where I'm coming from love plopped out of
the sky and poured out His life with me in mind.
And I can't count the number of times
I've passed Him

By
Passed Him
Over
Exemplified
The very actions that placed Him on that tree
The sin that had Him die for me
And I've been redeemed but it seems
I'm forever prone to
Depravity
And it's a cavity I can't escape
But He never ceases to lavish amazing grace
And this grace
Reaches down into the core of my mess
Cleansing every crevice
Leaving me
Sinless
And I don't get it
Why am I seen as righteous
When all that's within me is
Deceit
And
Darkness
But His light...

Oh His light
Penetrates the darkest of nights
Cracks my innermost being
Love;
Steadfast.
Beaming.
Heart
Beating.
Doubt
Retreating.
And
All I can do is sit and relish
In the greatest of
Joys
In the sweetest of presents
And His presence
Presents me with that which my soul most cherishes
So
One day,
I'll meet Him in the sky
Having poured out my life
With Him in mind.

"Greater love has no one than this: to lay down one's life for one's friends." John 15:13

"Oh you love ___? Would you die for it?" There's a running joke among a group of my friends concerning love. When one of us says we love something, and someone thinks it too strong a word, we question the extent of the love. "Oh you love pizza—but would you die for it?" The point we make is that love is a strong word, and to love something with sincerity requires a willingness to give something up as evidence of that love. Tangible love, the real deal and not the kind we use when referring to our favourite sports teams, is the kind that will act, and it is through that action that the love is truly demonstrated. Christ gave Himself up for us on the cross, this display showed us what real love looks like. If God was willing to give Himself up for us to show that He loves us, should we not readily do the same? God demonstrates love as an action, if we claim to love we must do likewise.

Romans 12:9-10, in the New Living Translation, urges us, "Don't just pretend to love others. Really love them. Hate what is wrong. Hold tightly to what is good. Love each other with genuine affection, and take delight in honouring each other." We might claim to love people, but we have to ask if the way we act towards them communicates this to be true. The two greatest commandments are to love God and love people (Matthew 22:36-40). Now Christ didn't die on the cross that we'd be perpetually indebted to Him, trying our best to follow a set of rules to somehow appease Him. His intentions weren't such that we'd spend all our days striving to prove our love and devotion back to Him, and though we joke about it, God doesn't require us to die a martyr's death in order to demonstrate the extent of our commitment. But still, love does necessarily require action.

So what then does it look like to love God and love people? Love is an act of devotion. When two people get married they promise to stay with one another through thick or thin, in sickness and in health, for richer or for poorer. Loving in both of these capacities looks similar. To love God takes us resolving to trust and stand with Him regardless of our circumstances. It requires a commitment to follow Him all the days of our life and live every day for Him. To love people requires putting them ahead of ourselves, it calls for active acts of forgiveness and self-sacrifice, treating them like Christ did us. It takes standing up against injustices and taking up the cause of the oppressed. This love knows no passivity, no fear; only a commitment to stay true and suffer long.

This kind of love is extremely difficult in our own strength, in fact it's entirely impossible. We do not possess in ourselves the capacity to fully and completely love like God does. Thankfully, the God who Himself is love is more than able and willing to empower us to love beyond our limitations. Spending time with the one who is love, learning what love looks like from His example, receiving His love: these things will enable us, make it impossible to not, love as He does. 1 John 1:19-21 says, "We love because he first loved us." With God's help, we are empowered to demonstrate our love for Him and others every day, giving Him continued thanks for who He is, and following His perfect example of love.

Unconventional

    This poem was birthed out of a conversation I had with a group of inspiring, beautiful ladies on a Monday evening. We were talking about a God that we barely comprehend and how amazing that is. How fabulous it is to serve a master so much bigger than ourselves. To know that our lives are entrusted in the hands of a being that does not answer to us, is not limited in the ways that we are and does not have reservations when expressing His love. He's predictable in that reality, we know that He will love us, we know He is kind and good; and yet we have no idea. He is so unconventional. He is not a God like any other, rather, He is one that has no need of us and no reason to love us and yet He does; completely. Without restraint. Wow, what a glorious reality.

So predictably kind
Yet so—
Unpredictable.
What kind of God would see a flawed heart like mine and love it in spite of itself?

He's
Unconventional
And it's incredible...
Cause I'm acquainted with a love that stretched its arms down through the span of time to draw me unto itself
Been given a gift undeserved sent before the foundations of the earth to woe me unto its grace
And I was once
Marred by the stench of death,
Scarred by my brokenness,
He
Met me with arms outstretched I'm drenched in peace.
And this hope runs deep;
Peace sets free,
Seen
Love tangibly,
And yet
What we now see is but a reflection of what will one day be face to face
But still I'm stricken and awestruck by just a glimpse of His grace.

Captivated by His expressions,
Of relentless affections
This God defies conventions
A love with no exceptions.
Exceptional
He's
Unconventional...

"To the LORD your God belong the heavens, even the highest heavens, the earth and everything in it. Yet the LORD set his affection on your forefathers and loved them, and he chose you, their descendants, above all the nations, as it is today." Deuteronomy 10:14-15

"For now we see only a reflection as in a mirror; then we shall see face to face. Now I know in part; then I shall know fully, even as I am fully known."
1 Corinthians 13:12

    We think we're pretty smart. We like to reason and understand and use our logic to make sense of the world around us. This is a useful, special feature of the human experience. There is such a value in being able to comprehend the things that impact our lives, and it's certainly a tremendous thing when we answer questions that perplexed the generations before us. The thing about God however, is that we can't actually get to that place with Him. We can't simply reason our way towards understanding. What we know about Him, what we will ever know about Him, will only really scratch the surface of the expanse that is He, and though on one hand He desires that we know Him, and takes pleasure in revealing Himself to us, we can and will never fully get it. There's a deep beauty that lies in this, the reality that the God of the Universe is so vast that we can't fathom Him. He's beyond us, in the best way possible. It means that He's bigger than us. It means that He's not on the same plane as our finite, flawed selves. This is great news because we are so limited. A God that is a real God, a God that rules over the galaxies and the cosmos, must be one that is not answerable to any of us.

While it could be unsettling to think about a vast, all-powerful being that we can't fully understand, we must remember the nature of our God. At the end of the day, our God is a good, loving one, and if there's one thing we should grasp as the base of His character, it's this: He loves us; unceasingly. He's good, He's big, He's powerful, He's all knowing, and He's *for us*. God knows all that there is to know and He has our best interests, for our eternal good, always at heart.

A passage of scripture that I find so incredibly comforting comes out of Romans 8:31-39:

> "What, then, shall we say in response to these things? If God is for us, who can be against us? He who did not spare his own Son, but gave him up for us all—how will he not also, along with him, graciously give us all things? Who will bring any charge against those whom God has chosen? It is God who justifies. Who then is the one who condemns? No one. Christ Jesus who died—more than that, who was raised to life—is at the right hand of God and is also interceding for us. Who shall separate us from the love of Christ? Shall trouble or hardship or persecution or famine or nakedness or danger or sword...
>
> For I am convinced that neither death nor life, neither angels nor demons, neither the present nor

the future, nor any powers, neither height nor depth, nor anything else in all creation, will be able to separate us from the love of God that is in Christ Jesus our Lord."

This is great news, whether we can fully grasp it or not. We serve a big God who loves us and we will never be separated from that burning, unconventional love.

Good Thing

    This poem is about searching for love when I was never intended to. It's about finally coming to understand that I was created not to seek out love but to be forever suspended in its truest, purest form.

    For a long time I was weighed down by the fact that I have a sorry history of romantic companionship. I'd thought there must be something wrong with me if at the age of twenty I've had no relationships to show. I'd felt like I needed the love of a man to fulfill me and prove that I'm of value, and that's a massive lie. Beyond even that, I thought love was my job to find.

    This poem makes me uncomfortable. The concept came from reflecting on the fact that myself and so many girls I know are constantly seeking out companionship and hoping to satisfy that ever innate desire for love. Of course this isn't a bad thing, but when it becomes an ultimate thing it becomes unhealthy and no human possesses the capacity to truly satisfy us. This poem is about the emptiness and dissatisfaction that ultimately leads to that revelation.

This poem makes me uncomfortable so I felt like it needed to be shared...

He who finds a wife finds a good thing...
And I used to be lost.
Searching to find something other than the love I've been freely given
Cause see before I was born I'd been handed a ring
Extended to me by a hanging king
But I
Remained blind to the sign right in front of me.
And before my eyes were clear
My four-eyes would forage for guys that'd have me hypnotized
Swayed by nice words and sweet lies
Liking the idea of sweet times
But in due time I'd crash from a sugar high.
Hiding I'd cry
Lonely inside
A life awry
Longing to find
Some good thing.
But all I got was something bad and ugly.

In bondage and lonely
Desperate for company
Determined to accompany the broken inside of me
Thought affection could fill my total depravity
And this wasn't a good thing.
And I adopted idols that took the form of tall, dark, and handsome
Unhealthy habits had my mind for ransom
My mind wandering off to matrimony before words were even exchanged
I'd wonder about exchanging vows and last names
Mind ablaze
Cause I wanted that good thing.
But that thing was never mine to find in the first place.
The first mistake:
Believing that good could be found from my own strength,
That love could be recognized by the frail heart in my own chest,
When love sacrificed itself to pay my debt
See I used to be lost.

And what I've found is that the search from the start was off,
Off base.
My job is to wait.
To be found.
So I'll stop seeking and running around,
Cause I've got love and He sacrificed
Life slayed for mine
In His Resurrection I'm found,
Found love in Christ.
And that's a good thing.

"Daughters of Jerusalem, I charge you: Do not arouse or awaken love until it so desires."
Song of Solomon 8:4

"He who finds a wife finds a good thing and obtains favor from the LORD." Proverbs 18:22 (ESV)

Love is a good thing. Very good in fact.

And yet so many people can attest to love gone awry, relationships ended in heartbreak, bliss turned to hatred in an instant. Romantic love is a delicate thing, emotionally charged, sensitive, and so often subject to our lust and selfishness. We've established that love is overwhelmingly the deepest soul craving that we possess. We were created to love love, and for good reason; it's a beautiful gift from God. Yet so often love doesn't pan out in the beautiful way it's supposed to. So often we abuse it, we take advantage of one another, use the people we are meant to care about for our own selfish gain. We exploit it, we demand it, or we fail to genuinely express it out of fear. All this is the sad result of our depravity apart from God. It's difficult for us to properly express love in the contexts that God created because so much of who we are is characterized by our self-seeking, sinful nature. It's so easy for us to look to love as a mechanism to fulfill ourselves rather than serve and honour others as we were originally intended to. We are so desperate for it that we act contemptibly, and in the process hurt the people around us as well as ourselves.

When God envisioned romantic love, He intended for it to be a mutually enriching, self-sacrificing, unconditional kind that reflects the love that He so beautifully pioneered. God's love is patient, He's loved each one of us long before we ever acknowledged or reciprocated that love. The love that we are meant to express is a patient kind, one that is willing to wait and that is gentle and long suffering. Rushing love is a mistake, forcing it is a disservice to the full, genuine blessing that it can be. God has placed the desire for relationship in most of us, but we must be willing to wait on His timing and trust that He has good intentions towards us, that He knows us and thus knows what is best. If we want successful relationships we have to keep love at the center. God is love, and He belongs as the central point of orientation, holding together all loves. God faithfully pursues us, and in all that we do we ought to pursue Him first, especially in regards to relationships.

It's a great thing to desire love, but at the end of the day we already have it in the God of the universe, we don't need to go searching for it. If and when we get romantic love, it's simply an additional, unmerited gift from a good, generous father.

"This is how we know what love is: Jesus Christ laid down his life for us. And we ought to lay down our lives for our brothers and sisters." 1 John 3:16

GRACE

Grace, as I've come to understand it, is one of the most beautiful concepts in the universe.

It brings me deep joy to think that we are treated with love and favour in spite of ourselves. In spite of our pride, and selfishness, and tendency to mess up. I can't say that I fully comprehend or understand why grace is extended to us, but what I do know is that it leaves me in awe.

"And if by grace, then it is no longer by works; if it were, grace would no longer be grace." Romans 11:6

Gratia

    This poem is the Gospel as simply as I've understood it. It's my attempt to sum up the most beautifully captivating love story ever told.

    God made mankind. We in our folly sinned against Him. He in His goodness created a way to bring us back into right relationship with Himself. He sent Jesus to die on the cross to pay a penalty that was not His. This sacrifice made it possible for us to be free, and through Christ's resurrection, through His triumph over death, we no longer have to suffer the consequences of sin, guilt, shame, or fear. If we would only call on the name of Jesus, and turn from our wicked ways, we can have the opportunity to know true joy, freedom, and life.

And so it begins and ends with abundant grace...
The story is simple as it is complex.
Dust formed.
Life.
Breath.
A people commit offense.

Loving God.
Transcends.
We're called to simply repent.
Turn.
Return.
His outstretched arms extend.
Love cascades.
Fear erased.
Sins once scarlet.
Spotless.

"When the woman saw that the fruit of the tree was good for food and pleasing to the eye, and also desirable for gaining wisdom, she took some and ate it. She also gave some to her husband, who was with her, and he ate it. Then the eyes of both of them were opened, and they realized they were naked; so they sewed fig leaves together and made coverings for themselves." Genesis 3:6-7

"And the free gift is not like the result of that one man's sin. For the judgment following one trespass brought condemnation, but the free gift following many trespasses brought justification." Romans 5:16

Humankind has inherited a sin nature that makes us enemies of God. When Adam and Eve ate the apple in the Garden of Eden, they rebelled against the Lord's command and thus sent us all into a spiral of sin and depravity. As a result, we are naturally separated from the perfect God of love, who has no affiliation with evil and cannot in His nature tolerate sin. What grace is then, is God's loving means of reconciling the tension between us and Himself.

First and foremost, we don't deserve it. There's no reason that we should get grace and we certainly did not earn it. This reality is precisely what makes grace grace; it can't be earned. On a fundamental level, grace can only be extended by an individual in a position of power to an undeserving, guilty party. This is to say that true grace is something that comes from God and something that only He is capable of extending. Someone shows mercy if they are owed a penalty by another, but instead of holding the guilty responsible, they resolve to withdraw the penalty that is due. What God's grace looks like takes this a step further. It looks like standing in the place of the guilty individual and rewarding them despite their wrong. God is capable of extending grace to each of us because He overflows with excessive, abundant love. Instead of simply pardoning our sins, He goes the extra mile and redeems us wholly. Making us wholly clean, wholly righteous, and wholly new. The Gospel or good news, is that Jesus Christ came to the earth to save us. He was crucified, died, and rose, taking our sin and conquering the grave once and for all. This was an act of love and supreme grace. We wronged Him and yet He paid the penalty of death, and nothing that we have done or ever will do will be able to repay Him. Thankfully, we don't have to. Through Christ's sacrifice we have the opportunity to return to right standing with God, to have our sins paid for when we acknowledge who Christ is and what He did. Grace like this is the grand narrative surrounding God's relation with mankind; it's a simple story of redemption, yet so vastly, intricately, glorious.

Unmerited Mercy

The woman caught in adultery.

As someone who grew up in the church I'd heard the story countless times, but at one moment, suddenly, as the word of God is so characteristic of, something resonated and I found myself dumbfounded by the reality of the grace of God.

I wondered what it must have been like to receive such as undeserved pardon, what would have come over her as she stood eye in eye with the creator of the universe and encountered pure love. What would her reaction have been? What would it have looked like? This poem is my attempt to peer into her mind and explore some of my questions. I hope it leaves you in awe of a God who is so quick to forgive and so ready to redeem. I hope it reminds you that you are never too far from grace. I hope you are able to see just a bit more of the character and nature of a God that knows you completely and never ceases to pursue you in love.

"Let him who is without sin cast the first stone."
Her accusers retreated,
There she stood with Jesus,
Alone.
Face to face
With the embodiment of grace
Not a trace of condemnation in His tone:
"Go,
and sin no more"
He spoke.
And I imagine it sent shivers of love down the shafts of her soul,
That on that day hope ricocheted through the core of her bones,
That the weight of his words made her broken heart whole,
That shame was silenced by the sentence alone;
Stagnant.
And I imagine...
At the sound of His voice life sprung through her pulse,
That her veins vibrated from the violence of love.
And I wonder...

Did this pronouncement send her trembling to her knees?
Was she baffled and broken by the weight of His speech?
Steeped;
Deep;
In His shower of peace.
Drowning;
Drenched;
In love endlessly.
Free;
Freed;
Unmerited mercy.

"Then Jesus stood up again and said to the woman, 'Where are your accusers? Didn't even one of them condemn you?'
'No, Lord,' she said.
And Jesus said, 'Neither do I. Go and sin no more.'"
John 8:10-11

Gifts are delightful. There's something thoroughly heartwarming about receiving a symbol of another's affection for you, something special about knowing that they'd give with no expectation of getting anything in return. When parents give gifts to their children, they don't do so because they expect to get anything back; they do it to see the thrill, the delight, the ecstasy on the face of the child that they adore. The grace of God is a gift of this sort. It is a grace that gives in a pure, nonsensical way and it does so with no apologies and no hidden motives.

    In the story of the woman caught in adultery, Jesus extended grace to her that only He was capable of giving. The religious leaders of the day found this woman in the act of adultery, they brought her before Jesus, ready to sentence her to death, but instead He rebuked them with a simple admission. He declared that anyone there who was sinless had permission to enact judgement. Each one of them walked away, aware that they themselves were not blameless, were by no means in the position to point a finger at her. But Jesus, He who was in fact without sin, even in His justified perfection abstained from carrying out the penalty. Instead, He enabled her to move forward with the permission to turn from her life of sin. His act of grace would have bought for her the license to be better, to choose life over death and move forward to a higher calling having received a gift of perfect love. Adorned with the knowledge that she was not sentenced by her wrongs, that she wouldn't have to carry around the weight of her guilt, but was instead forgiven, she would have been equipped to live a life of freedom. This is what grace does: it liberates us to not just do better but to actually be better. When our sins are handed over to God they are payed for, God no longer sees us as sinful but instead as He sees Jesus: blameless and righteous. 2 Corinthians 5:21 tells us that "God made him who had no sin to be sin for us, so that in him we might become the righteousness of God." When we accept Christ's atoning sacrifice on the cross, He lifts from us the title of sinner and calls us friends of God. We are made new, and so much like the woman caught in adultery, we too can leave our lives of sin empowered by God's strength. It is out of this place alone, understanding God's unmerited mercy towards us, that we are able to walk out the new identity we have, showcasing our reality as the righteousness of God.

Grace

This poem was birthed from reflecting on some of my favourite verses in all of scripture. The first explains that we've been given grace in the place of grace already given. That our good God is so ready, so ever willing to lavish upon us more and more and more grace. The other says that where sin abounds, grace abounds all the more. In other words, God's grace is entirely infinite, cannot and does not come to an end.

These truths are so profound, so liberating, so completely, thoroughly, beautiful. I pray that in reading this the reality of grace comes to life before your eyes. I pray it'd reach the depths of your soul in a fresh way. Grace is incredible, and it's irrevocably yours to receive.

Grace
In the place of grace already given
Should've been dead
But He's already risen
Granted

His rights for the wrongs I committed,
Should've had debt but my sins He's acquitted
Prison
My sentence but that phrase resubmitted
Should've been worthless but that charge now fictitious
Value and purpose
Cause my life's been commissioned
He did it
Not my works but His gift it
Is finished
Surpassing love so relentless
I'm finished
The end of me the beginning
Can't count it
Surpassing joy so infinite
I'm finished
Newly made in His image
His presence
Grace abounds I just relish
His fullness
Grace for grace without merit

"Out of his fullness we have all received grace in place of grace already given." John 1:16

"Now the law came in to increase the trespass, but where sin increased, grace abounded all the more." Romans 5:20 (ESV)

It's hard to imagine something inexhaustible. We're quite familiar with limitations. We understand the confines of only being capable of so much, of running out of energy, growing tired, becoming weak. We see in finite terms, and so to say that something could exist that does not come to an end is a difficult concept to grapple with. When we think about the universe, or the depths of the sea, we get a sort of idea of something that continues and extends without an end. Even still, these concepts are beyond us. When it comes to the grace of God, it is literally boundless. God Himself has no beginning and no end, and so His ability to extend goodness towards us does and can not end. We get grace in the place of grace that we've been previously given. Grace and mercy anew every morning, continually lavished from His inexhaustible wells.

We humans are imperfect. We make mistakes, we go back on our word, we neglect to fulfil promises, and so much more. When it comes to relating to God, we have an incredible aptitude for messing up. We forsake Him, we sin against Him; we have no real potential to do anything but wrong Him. Thankfully, His grace abounds. It is so full, so everlasting that there's nothing we can do that is beyond it. There's a common idiom that speaks about "falling from grace", suggesting that as a result of our sin we can get on God's bad side in a sort of indefinite way. The reality however, is that that's impossible; you can only ever fall deeper and deeper into the grace of God. It's boundless. This is amazing news. This is news that frees us up to live without fear of being "too far gone". At the same time it is by no means a license to sin; Romans 6:1-2 (NKJV) puts in perfectly when it asks, "What shall we say then? Shall we continue in sin that grace may abound? Certainly not! How shall we who died to sin live any longer in it?" Instead, understanding grace lets us know that God in His goodness is trustworthy to keep us in right standing with Himself. The Bible says that He is faithful to complete the work that he began in us (Philippians 1:6). We can't fall from grace because He carries us. The beautiful reality is that God is not intimidated by our humanness, He simply looks at us through grace-colored glasses, calling us further and deeper into the fullness of His divinity.

Words

    This poem was birthed upon reflecting on the fact that words carry weight. The things we say have the capacity to harm or to heal. Most of us can recall moments in our lives when things others said to or about us, for better or worse, had a lasting impact on our perspective. For me, I can remember, vividly, words that have been directed at me to crush me, phrases yielded by insensitive tongues that didn't care about the implications of what they said. Didn't concern themselves with the hurt they would cause. On the other hand, words of affirmation have built me up in ways I can hardly explain.

    With this poem, I was expressing my desire that the things I say for the rest of my days would always fall into the second category. That I would not use words to destroy or tear down but always to exhort. Beyond this though, I pray that my words would always point to a source of joy and life far bigger that I. That the things I say always be laced with grace, and as such, you'd come to know grace Himself.

Words have the power to change lives
And I say this simply because words changed mine
And so I hope that the words I write always build up
That when I'm gone the message that's left would always edify.
I pray that my quotes be laced with the grace I confess to know
I pray that what's always conveyed is the truth that brings hope
I hope my words rewrite the wrongs that other words wrote
I hope what I say gives way to a joy you've never known
Oh that my words would bring peace
That people would experience love with every word I speak
That as I project my speech your chains would release
That as my sentences progress doubt and fear would retreat
I want words that bring healing
Mend broken pieces
Would they clothe you with comfort

Cure your diseases
Rhymes full of freedom
Flows full of meaning
My wish is that you're washed by the love of
Jesus
Jesus.
The Word.
In the beginning was the word.
Cause God so loved the world that He gave the word
His only child
And that Word changed my life.
So would my phrases give praises to the God of all ages
Would His words litter my lips and redirect gazes
Towards the word that transcends mine
Would they point to the divine.
Words.
Word.
Life.

"In the beginning was the Word, and the Word was with God, and the Word was God. He was in the beginning with God. All things were made through him, and without him was not any thing made that was made. In him was life, and the life was the light of men. The light shines in the darkness, and the darkness has not overcome it." John 1:1-5

"I hate, I despise your religious festivals;
  your assemblies are a stench to me.
Even though you bring me burnt offerings and grain offerings,
  I will not accept them.
Though you bring choice fellowship offerings,
  I will have no regard for them.
Away with the noise of your songs!
  I will not listen to the music of your harps.
But let justice roll on like a river,
  righteousness like a never-failing stream!"
Amos 5:21-24

"Do not let any unwholesome talk come out of your mouths, but only what is helpful for building others up according to their needs, that it may benefit those who listen." Ephesians 4:29

Having received the grace of God, we get to be vessels that extend His overflowing, permeating mercies to a world so in need of it. Words are significant. They have immense power to be weapons of destruction or those of restoration. With words God spoke the universe into existence, with His declaration He announced how He would redeem the world after Adam and Eve's slip up in the garden, with words He established His promise to Abraham and His descendants. Just as God's words carry immense power, our words can similarly be tools to create or tear down. Psalms 18:21 (ESV) says that "death and life are in the power of the tongue". When we speak, we project either life or death, we either build up or bring down those around us.

Our social media age is one where people are quick to throw words. With little repercussions in networks filled with billions of people, it can be so easy to communicate in ways that devalue, discourage, or undermine our common humanity. A verse that I find so profound, one that always brings me to a place of self-examination, is Luke 6:45. It explains that "the good person out of the good treasure of his heart produces good, and the evil person out of his evil treasure produces evil, for out of the abundance of the heart his mouth speaks." This is to say that we naturally produce that which is in our hearts. That if we are full of hatred we speak to people out of hate, but if we are full of love and grace then our speech will reflect this in a practical way. We should know that the things that we say are significant. When we speak we participate in God's extension of grace, mercy, and justice upon humankind. We get to be a part of the outpouring of His love when we are filled with it and move forward to overflow onto others. Our speech ought to be the kind that stands up against abuses and sets people free. We should use our words to fight for rights and give life; to be the voices that stand up for the oppressed and mistreated in our world.

In the Gospels, Jesus is continually referred to as the Word. John 1:14 says that "the Word" became flesh, and dwelt among us, referencing Christ's birth as a human not unlike ourselves. When we speak, we have the opportunity to use words that reflect the essence and heartbeat of the Word, to put it differently, as we communicate in our various spheres, our use of language can point back to the love, goodness, and grace of God. 2 Corinthians 5:19-20 explains that "He has committed to us the message of reconciliation. We are therefore Christ's ambassadors, as though God were making his appeal through us." This is an incredible assignment that we get to carry out: speaking life into places that are dead and dying and pointing back to who God is. As with love we learn to extend grace when we spend time understanding the grace that God has extended to each of us, allowing us to better display it to those around us. God said let there be light, and there was light. The things we say can similarly bright light to a dark world around us.

Slow Dancing with Sovereignty

    I wrote this poem on my last birthday. Twenty came extremely quickly. Sometimes I feel like I blinked through the uncomfortable, unpleasant teen years and plunged into adulthood, though it seldom felt like it at the time.

    I found myself extremely reflexive, as I perhaps too often am, and couldn't help but think about the countless ways that God's displayed His grace in my life. I've certainly done nothing to deserve my fate, I could have been born into a society that murders their young daughters or sells them into the sex trade. I could've been raised in a culture that enslaves women of color or refuses them an education. I could've been born in tumultuous times of war and suffered the displacement of so many refugees today. All this would have been horrific, and I'm grateful for the freedom that I have, but more than anything else, I'm so blessed to know and be known by God. To have from a young age been introduced to that which is unconditional acceptance, love, favour, and grace; to have in recent years begun to understand what that means.

My life has been a whirlwind of happy days of birth and good gifts but it has so little to do with what I own and so much to do with who has known me all along. My prayer is that this be true for each one of you.

Twenty.
My life has been a whirlwind of grace and faith
expressing themselves in the stillness and chaos alike.
I've been at peace and broken, in pieces and floating,
My heart's beat and swollen and I pray this doesn't
change for years to come.
I'm never in control, mostly unsure, at moments
insecure, but I'm learning more and more the
blessing of this reality.
I never want to take any of my blessings casually.
I want to embrace my vulnerability,
I'd like to learn to love unconditionally.
Eventually,
I'll see the fruit of my efforts come to fruition
I'll see my dreams reach their final destination

Until then
I will flourish by the still waters where I'm planted
I will give thanks and take no day for granted
At twenty,
For eternity,
I'll be slow dancing with sovereignty.

"May the God of hope fill you with all joy and peace as you trust in him, so that you may overflow with hope by the power of the Holy Spirit." Romans 15:13

"Now may the Lord of peace himself give you peace at all times and in every way... The grace of our Lord Jesus Christ be with you all." 2 Thessalonians 3:16, 18

    Grace changes everything. Seeing the hand of God, recognizing His graces upon our lives, naturally puts us in a place of awe and gratitude towards Him. James 1:17 says that "every good and perfect gift is from above, coming down from the Father of the heavenly lights, who does not change like shifting shadows." Every time we receive something good, it is a gracious gift from our heavenly father. God is good to us because He is good, and so we as His children get to reap the benefits of His generosity. It's our inheritance, and when we sit back and think about our lives, each of us, despite the hardships and difficulties that we have inevitably faced, can recognize common graces of God. Family, friendships, sunshine, good food: all of these things are a result of God's providence, supplying us with things that sustain us and even those that go beyond our immediate needs. And yet, God's grace should not be simplified to just providing for us, billions of people don't have their basic needs met but God still extends grace to them. Even when famine hits, or floods pillage towns and countries, we that know Him get to be a part of extending grace. We get to use the resources and means we've been given to love and bless others. As we freely receive God's grace, we get to give it freely, being partakers in His incredible process of restoration. God's joy and peace are the direct result of understanding His grace, and in understanding His grace, we become distributors of it, filled in a way that leaves us no choice but to care for people and demonstrate the grace that we've been shown. Now "may God give you more and more grace and peace as you grow in your knowledge of God and Jesus our Lord" (2 Peter 1:2 NLT).

"For the grace of God has appeared that offers salvation to all people." Titus 2:11

FREEDOM

It took me a long time to feel free.

In fact, I'd lived in captivity for far longer than I'd ever known peace. For a long time I lived weighed down by fear and doubt and until I saw love and grace in a tangible way I existed in a state of captivity. Enslaved by a mentality of fear. One day I finally felt the Lord whisper the most comforting words over me. He said simply, "Get free".

"So if the Son sets you free, you will be free indeed."
John 8:36

Abide

Abide is about finding comfort, refuge, and peace in a God that is so near and so present. It's about the ultimate source of strength that lies in His wide, ready arms.

I wrote this poem simply thinking about what God might say to one of us in a time of turmoil or strife. If He could communicate something to us in the midst of our stress, what would it be? Would He give us a list of reasons why our worry was unwarranted, would He scold us for having such little faith, or would He simply remind us to rest in Him? To lay aside our concerns for some brief moments of solace. Would He remind us of who He is and that we are His? I think He would. I think He'd speak truths gently over us until we were lulled into the depths of His grace and freedom. I pray you'd forever reside in that place.

Abide.
In my outstretched arms
Hide.
Seek

&
Find.
Light.
My child
Dine.
Receive what's
Mine.
I've paid the
Fine.
Abundant
Life.
In me
Abide.

"He who dwells in the secret place of the Most High
Shall abide under the shadow of the Almighty.
I will say of the Lord, "He is my refuge and my
fortress; My God, in Him I will trust."
Psalm 91:1-2 (NKJV)

"Be anxious for nothing, but in everything by prayer
and supplication, with thanksgiving, let your requests
be made known to God; and the peace of God, which

surpasses all understanding, will guard your hearts and minds through Christ Jesus."
Philippians 4:6-7 (NKJV)

"Come to Me, all you who labor and are heavy laden, and I will give you rest. Take My yoke upon you and learn from Me, for I am gentle and lowly in heart, and you will find rest for your souls. For My yoke is easy and My burden is light." Matthew 11:28-31 (NKJV)

There is so much freedom in surrender. We can often feel like we have to deal with our messes, that if we don't fret or worry incessantly they will never go away. It's entirely counter-intuitive to think that in giving up control, in ceasing to try, it's possible to arrive at a place where our concerns are actually handled. But this is what God promises; He assures us that in giving up our constant strain, in handing Him our worries, we will get to a place of peace and freedom through Him. Yes, it goes against our intuition, Philippians 4 literally states that the peace of God surpasses *all understanding*. We don't get it, we can't, and we're not supposed to. What we need to get is that God is mighty, He's above our issues, no matter how massive and overwhelming they might seem. He's not phased. All He ever is is in control and loving and full of grace and it's in understanding this that we get to finally find rest. Seeing God for who He is, realizing that He is ultimately sovereign over every problem we will ever face, puts everything else into perspective.

Resting can be difficult, especially when we're accustomed to carrying the weight of our burdens. It's difficult to let go, we can glean a distorted kind of comfort from holding on to our woes. But until we receive God's rest, until we let Him shoulder our burdens, we can't truly begin to combat anything that comes our way. At some point we have to lay it all down, at some point we have to take up His rest and trust Him. It's in this surrender, in this laying down, that we receive freedom.

Marked

I don't know if I've ever written a more deeply personal poem than this one. I recently performed it at an event at my university and remember feeling so odd about the fact that I was baring my soul before a room full of mostly complete strangers. What was odd wasn't my willingness to do so it but how necessary it felt. How important it was that I be honest about the fact that I've struggled to see myself as worthwhile and deserving of love because—who hasn't? What made it so fundamentally important though, was the fact that I wasn't simply getting it off my chest in an attempt to generate sympathy, I'm not really one for commiseration, but rather I was hoping, and still am, that my vulnerability would open up the floor for you to confront some of the ways that you've believed lies about who you are and can be. More than that, I pray that you'd begin to understand who you are, not as others see you or even as you see yourself, but rather as your Father in Heaven does. That He'd reveal to you the truth of your identity as a son or daughter of the Most High. My prayer is that you'd receive a full revelation of your calling and of the true you, made in God's image and infinitely known and loved.

It's woven into her sleeves
The marks of the person she
Never asked to be
Sown into the very fabric of her being
She
Can't escape the trace of identity
She
Can't erase the mark of race
Try as she may it shows on her face
And she
Struggles to believe in the beauty others claim to see.
Plagued
With a blackness of skin
She's
Blessed by the sting of melanin
And she
Navigates a foreign world
Struggles to endure
Standards unattainable that were never meant for her:

Straight hair,
Light skin,
Too thick,
Or
Too thin?
She
Finds herself burdened by
The lies she's fed day and night
Scrolls down her feed and
Eats up images that fail to nourish the empty
Her stomach churns as photos stream
A stream of tears become familiarity
So she
Sculpts the flawed parts of herself
Covers up the scars and buffs away the mess
Blurs the lines and conceals the rest
Makeup to mask the brokenness
But
If she only knew she was made up
Of pieces of divinity
Strewn together by hands that have loved her for eternity
Intricately strung,

Lavished with love,
She doesn't have to cover up.
See
She's
Already received a prize she could not believe
Bought for a price that no man can exceed
So
In the midst of pain
Her fear fades away
Her scars become a sonnet
Her tears fail to stay
She realizes
That the chocolate of her skin
Possesses beauty therein
That her dark is marked as radiant as stars
See
Her figure was traced
Her pigment was placed
By the arms of grace.

"For you created my inmost being;
 you knit me together in my mother's womb.

I praise you because I am fearfully and wonderfully made;
  your works are wonderful,
  I know that full well.
My frame was not hidden from you
  when I was made in the secret place,
  when I was woven together in the depths of the earth.
Your eyes saw my unformed body;
  all the days ordained for me were written in your book
  before one of them came to be.
How precious to me are your thoughts, God!
  How vast is the sum of them!
Were I to count them,
  they would outnumber the grains of sand"
Psalm 139: 13-18

    Our identities are something that we all have to wrestle with. We hear voices every day, some from those that we know, some from the world around us, and an overwhelming number from ourselves. We navigate the spaces we live in trying to determine what our place is. What role do we ultimately play? Where do we fit in? We have the challenge of making sense of intersecting and overlapping, at times contradictory standards, and as a result we are apt to get lost and buy into the wrong information. A lot of the time we find ourselves believing lies about our identities. We allow those with no right or authority to feed us false information about who we are or who we should be. We think that we are not valuable because we don't measure up to expectations of intellect, beauty, creativity, or on the other hand, if we do, we develop a sense of pride and grow conceited. It's difficult for us to have a balanced perception of ourselves because we see through distorted narratives, constructs that set us up to fail with standards that were never fitting for us in the first place.

We may not know who we are, but God does; completely. He made us and is aware of every little nuance, quirk, and imperfection that constitutes our person. Psalm 139 is a beautiful, intimate expression of God's relationship to the writer David, and further, to each one of us. It speaks about how there is nowhere we can go where God doesn't see us. It tells of how He knows us all together, how He knitted us together long before we were ever planned or thought up. It says that we were beautifully and wonderfully made, crafted by a designer that took great delight in whom He created. Knowing this, realizing that we were purposed and adored long before we ever came to be, is one of the fullest, most beautiful truths to grab hold of.

In the book of Genesis, God took dirt and breathed in it the breath of life and thus humankind was birthed. It says in chapter 1 verse 27 that "God created mankind in his own image, in the image of God he created them; male and female he created them." God made us in His image. This means that we are precious and magnificent creations. Somewhere along the line though, we bought lies that told us otherwise. These lies have taken us away from the truth of who we are: loved, precious, image bearers of divinity, and we've been deeply hurt as a result. Rather than living freely, embracing our unique, God-made identities, we fall into the trap of shrinking or changing who we've been made to be. God's truths are the only remedy. Until we truly, sincerely understand that we are worthwhile in His eyes, and that He loves and cares for us, we will never have a healthy view of ourselves. Instead we will live puffed up or destroyed by the voices around us. When we finally discern God's voice, when we finally hear Him tell us who we are, all others will fade into the shadows. There is incredible freedom in seeing that each of us was designed to reflect the glory of God. That He sees me and you and everyone around us as beautifully made regardless of popular opinion. His voice is the truest. His voice rings the loudest. His voice alone brings freedom.

Remember

This is a piece about discontentment. It's about feeling as though life in the now is somehow sub-par in comparison with the ever-elusive future. It's about being trapped in a cycle of believing that what you have isn't quite enough and if you only had this or that then, you'd be satisfied—

This is a trap. This is a lie that will leave you forever upset and consistently steal your joy. I've learnt this because I've experienced it happen. I've been subject to the despair of the "what if", of rushing through a season just wanting what was next and failing to learn from the present. It's tragic, a real disservice to the value of learning as you go, of growing through the misfortunes and curve balls as they arise. I believe now, truly, that there is something to be learnt in each and every circumstance of life, that there's purpose whether or not we fully grasp it in all that we encounter.

I profess to believe in a big God, and if this is true, I must trust in His timing. I must get to a place where I believe that He is completely sovereign, that everything occurs in time as it's supposed to and for a reason. I pray that both you and I would be firmly rooted in this place.

I'm trying to remember to remember
To learn to love where I'm at.
To appreciate the fact
That I can remember
That where I was last December isn't where I'm at today
That I experience life anew everyday
That everyday possesses individual grace
That that grace is laced with more in its place
But sometimes that's hard to remember.
Cause the next season always seems better:
Summer falls into winds that leave me bitter,
Autumn grows sour by the prospect of winter,
Wondering soul springs up streams,
Wandering my mind into dreams
And these—
Make it hard to remember.
But I wish I'd wake up

Understand that what I have now is more than enough
That I'm continually lavished with unceasing love
That the reason I'm here is ordained from above
Orchestrated and seen,
The seeds I plant now establish the garden to be
If only I'd remember.
That time's hand moves independent of me
That my experience now is but a speck in the light of eternity
In a flash.
These moments now will be but a memory
At last.
That which I'm looking toward will come to be
Indeed;
I must remember the brevity.
This too shall pass inevitably.
Would I learn to cherish the subtleties
Embrace the blessing of uncertainty
For certainly—
The present is best wasted dwelling on tomorrow's joys;

Gifts and sorrows coexist in each phase of life's exploit.
I need to remember to remember.
Would I learn to surrender.
Cause today won't last forever...

"And don't be wishing you were someplace else or with someone else. Where you are right now is God's place for you. Live and obey and love and believe right there." 1 Corinthians 7:17 (MSG)

"And we know that in all things God works for the good of those who love him, who have been called according to his purpose." Romans 8:28

Trying to chase the future is a snare, it's always in front of us, it's intangible; it never actually arrives. There's a real temptation to look to what's ahead of us with an unhealthy anticipation, anxiously waiting for the things that we are so sure will finally bring us to a place of satisfaction. We expect that if we just get that next thing, then we will be happy. The issue is that this is hardly the case, our futures never pan out the way we think they will, for better or worse. Disappointment arises, things fall through, and we find ourselves dissatisfied seeing that which we thought would bring ultimate contentment dissolve before our eyes.

It's a beautiful thing to dream, truly, but if we live lives ever focused on what we hope will one day happen, we will miss out on the graces that exist only in the now. Things occur as they do, and in the time that they do, according to God's will. When we fail to trust His timeline for our lives we miss out on finding peace in each stage that we are in. Moreover, we undermine the sovereignty of God when we question why things aren't happening as we'd like them to. Focusing on the future takes our attention off the things that God intends to teach us precisely where we are. It strips from us the ability to enjoy the fullness of our present blessings. We can't see God's active, present hand when we dwell only on elusive "what ifs"; there is no freedom in believing that our lives will be worthwhile only after we've reached certain milestones. It's an impossible chase set up to fail us; we will never get to where we think we ought to be.

Freedom comes only when we begin to recognize God in every aspect of our lives; when we develop hearts that are grateful, eyes that see Him, and minds that trust that He has our futures taken care of.

Free

    This poem came after being surrounded by people that looked like me but still feeling out of place.

    It's about finally learning that giving myself is all I've ever been called to. It's about learning that God uses us in our weakness. It's about learning to be free.

    My deepest revelation of freedom took place in the heart of a refugee camp. I stood amidst thousands of children that looked not unlike myself, hungry, displaced, and weary, and couldn't make sense of why God would place me there with so little to offer. I cried. I cried out to God to use me, and though I'd prayed this prayer before, this time it was different. God use *me*, as in me, as I am, with all I can offer in myself. Within minutes, and from that moment on, God showed me that that was possible. That me, with no particular ability, could minister in a profound way: by being who He has created me to be.

    That day I was given, and finally received, the freedom to be me. The revelation of this truth was incredible, and I am so in awe of a God that sees me as valuable despite my limited credentials. I was loosed to minister out of a place of joy, simply receiving God's love and allowing it to flow out of me. I don't think there's a higher calling in all of the universe. I don't believe there's a deeper, fuller truth. I pray you'd receive a similar vision.

Invisible
It seems.
"MUZUNGUS!"
They scream
I walk by unseen
Movements discreet
As they move what proceeds is hundreds of small feet
Features they chase not present in me
I sigh
Exhaling deeply
"Father use me"
A phrase repeated
Routine
But today its tones sound differently
"Father use me"
As I am
Simply

All I have
And I hear Him whisper words so sweet
"My child,
Your individuality
Is my glory"
Myself
Is all you've ever asked me to be
"My daughter,
You're seen
Walk forth in my peace
You're loved endlessly
Be free"

"It is for freedom that Christ has set us free. Stand firm, then, and do not let yourselves be burdened again by a yoke of slavery." Galatians 5:1

"In my anguish I cried to the LORD, and he answered by setting me free." Psalm 118:5

We can recognize that we were made in the image of God, but it's another thing to learn how to live out our identities day by day. Understanding that God made us is step one, and it's an incredible, crucial step. It is only when equipped with the knowledge of *imago dei* that we can move forward proudly bearing God's image. The next step, and one that is imperative, is coming to understand who He's uniquely crafted us to be and what that means for our lives. Each one of us is different. We have gifts and talents and aptitudes that are distinctly our own. When we gain the revelation that our lives were purposed, and not an accident, we become free to live seeing ourselves as valuable. It is from this place that we learn to freely be ourselves, showcasing the immense, diversely creative, power of God.

God brings with Him a felt, tangible freedom. "Now the Lord is the Spirit, and where the Spirit of the Lord is, there is freedom." When we spend time in His presence we begin to experience His freedom in greater doses, but it goes a step further: "And we all, who with unveiled faces contemplate the Lord's glory, are being transformed into his image with ever-increasing glory, which comes from the Lord, who is the Spirit" (2 Corinthians 3:17-18). This means that as we spend time in God's presence we grab hold of the ability to look more like Him, to more intensely reflect who He is. God's presence makes us free, and it makes it more and more possible to come to understand our ultimate purpose in life; to reflect His glory, and to point people to Him. We were made in His image, somewhere along the line we lost hold of that reality, but in knowing Christ He brings us back to the revelation of ourselves. A verse that I deeply love comes out of Acts 17:28, it explains that "in him we live and move and have our being" that "we are his offspring." It is in God that we live; it is in Him that we become all that we are. He's made us individually and it is through Him that we receive the ability to be all that we can be. We are His offspring, when we learn who He is we learn who we are, and conversely, as we live out our identities, we showcase who He is to the world around us.

Nostalgia

    This is a poem about learning to grieve the past and leave it there. It's about learning that dwelling on what was can be paralyzing and painful. It's about recognizing the incredible, heart-wrenching, beautiful, broken memories and being brave enough to move forward understanding that there are new mercies and joys every morning.

    There's a deep irony in that just a few months ago, I was struggling to be content in my present state and wanted with everything to leap into what I perceived to be the glorious future. Fast forward to now, and I look to the past with esteem like no other. I remember days basking in God's grace and want to get back to that place.

    For me, the lesson here is that you will rob yourself of every possible hope of joy if you dwell on either what was or what you think is to come. Fulfillment and freedom are possible only in the realm of counting your blessings and moving forward. The past is a beautiful place, the future a wondrous mystery, but we were never meant to live in either. I'm still in the process of learning this. I pray you'd receive a revelation far deeper than mine.

...Cause I could reminisce for days about the way that things have changed
How nothing stays the same
Think back to the good ol-days
Of moments long forgotten
Times that tic-tick-tocked away
Talks that raced away the clock
Chased the rays...
But as the sun crept with it was erased
Sunsets
It's like one day I rose to find
That rise and shine
Passed by in my mind
And now it's all ablaze
And all that's left are memories of what was
Reminders of things we'd done
Who I hoped I'd become
And in comparison the present always seems to pale
Today's sweets seldom seem a treat
The trick of reminiscing

It's like a whirlwind of second guessing
And I think there's a certain fondness to shame
A nostalgia in pain
Cause my mind replays these memories again and again
Been stuck
In the mire and muck
Of what was
But not today.
Today I will remain grateful
For the gift of the present is best served content
So I'll count my blessings til today is spent
And when I look back at the past
I'll smile and sigh and laugh
Looking forward to the future knowing those joys won't be my last

"Not that I have already obtained all this, or have already arrived at my goal, but I press on to take hold of that for which Christ Jesus took hold of me. Brothers and sisters, I do not consider myself yet to have taken hold of it. But one thing I do: Forgetting what is behind and straining toward what is ahead, I

press on toward the goal to win the prize for which God has called me heavenward in Christ Jesus."
Philippians 3:12-14

"I am not saying this because I am in need, for I have learned to be content whatever the circumstances. I know what it is to be in need, and I know what it is to have plenty. I have learned the secret of being content in any and every situation, whether well fed or hungry, whether living in plenty or in want. I can do all this through him who gives me strength."
Philippians 4:11-13

Just as living our lives fixed on an ever-perishing picture of the future poses a threat to our ultimate joy, living in the past does much to rob us of peace. When we find ourselves in circumstances that we are unhappy with, it can be tempting to look back to times when things were going well; the glory days of high school or college, our childhoods, or just generic moments when we felt on top. Life, even on a moment to moment basis, is full of ups and downs. So much of what goes on around us is outside of our control, and as a result, hard times, times of conflict, tension, or difficulty are sure to arise eventually, even often. It's tempting to retreat into recollections of better times, but if we stay there, we do ourselves a disservice.

Comparison is the thief of joy. Many of us understand this concept when it comes to comparing our lives or circumstances with those of others, but we so often fail to realize that it holds true in our own experiences. We put ourselves in bondage when we allow our pasts to influence our present. This is the case when we fail to let go of things we've done that we regret or feel ashamed of, of past hurts or pain, as well as when we cling too tightly to the memories that we cherish or hold dear. If we ever wish to feel free, if we ever wish to have joy in our lives, we have to develop a balanced view of where we've been, where we are, and where, by God's grace, we are going.

In the book of Philippians, Paul explores how he's found contentment learning to lay aside his circumstances and press on. He relies on Christ in every stage of life. "One thing I do: Forgetting what is behind and straining toward what is ahead, I press on toward the goal to win the prize for which God has called me". He moves forward, not ignoring what he has and what he's been given, but choosing to only recognize God in the midst of it all. Similarly, in a verse that many are familiar with, Paul makes a powerful assertion: "I can do all things through Christ who gives me strength". In context, Paul is saying that regardless of his circumstances, he has God's strength to carry him through. He says that whether well fed or hungry, whether living in plenty or in want, he relies solely on Christ, looking to Him for ultimate peace and comfort. This is what joy looks like, fully independent of our circumstances and rooted squarely in the constant goodness of God. Freedom and contentment come only in grabbing hold of this revelation. See we have access to surpassing satisfaction. We can come to know overflowing joy, overflowing peace, and complete freedom. This reality is achieved only in seeing Christ in all of our circumstances, in pressing forward, in understanding that in every stage He is present, and that His goodness is not exclusive to any particular time or place.

"Now the Lord is the Spirit, and where the Spirit of the Lord is, there is freedom." 2 Corinthians 3:17

FAITH

Faith is a plunge.

I write about faith not as an expert in belief but as someone who has learned through trials how to hold on. How to stand despite the mess that life so often shows itself to be. Faith is the endurance to trust and the trust to endure. It's standing on the edge of a cliff and embracing the mystery that awaits. It's believing that love, grace, and freedom are coming your way. It's the breathless, exhilarating, eye-opening point when it all becomes real.

"Now faith is being sure of what we hope for and certain of what we do not see." Hebrews 11:1

Swim

This piece is about leaping into the unknown, into the destiny that awaits on the other side of surrender, when following Christ finally becomes more that just lip service. It's about staring doubt in the face and moving forward in obedience. It's about the freedom that can only be found through faith.

I don't believe we ever arrive in our journey of faith. It's simply a constant, daily process of trusting God, leaning not on our own understanding, but instead leaning into Him. It's believing that He's trustworthy and good and that what He says is true. It's a continual, deliberate swim. Never stop swimming.

My toes are wet. But just the tips. My soles exposed. Ankles cold. I'm going in. I guess it's time. Wading through the lies. Moving past the tide. Knees deep. Knee deep in grace. Faith. Warm embrace. Splashed face. Waist in. Cause I've wasted time waiting. Fear fading. Steps blatant. Doubt quaking. Vacant. Shoulders. Head. No hesitation.

Dive.
Head first into grace so great
It
Penetrates and invades all my spaces
Will I sink? Will I swim?
Submerge.
Surfacing.
Emerge…
Breathe love in.

"But Jesus immediately said to them: 'Take courage! It is I. Don't be afraid.'
'Lord, if it's you," Peter replied, "tell me to come to you on the water.
'Come,' he said.
Then Peter got down out of the boat, walked on the water and came toward Jesus. But when he saw the wind, he was afraid and, beginning to sink, cried out, 'Lord, save me!'
Immediately Jesus reached out his hand and caught him. You of little faith,' he said, why did you doubt?'"
Matthew 14:27-31

Faith, much like love, is best treated as a verb. It requires action. It is useful only when exercised. To say that you believe in something is to say that you would rely on it through and through, that you would bet your life on it, continue to pursue it, stand up for it, even when everything else around you failed. Real faith, like love too, calls for a certain abandonment, a dying to self that can come only in trusting that you are ultimately and entirely in good hands. When Jesus called Peter out onto the water He was asking him to trust Him. He was commissioning him to focus not on his surroundings but wholly on Jesus' ability to provide. Looking at Jesus, Peter stood firmly upon the water, sustained by a faith that made the impossible possible. The laws of physics crumbled at the mercy of an ordinary man who believed in a big God, one willing to step out and demonstrate that He who he served was all powerful to carry him despite the storms that raged. Peter's downfall occurred when he took his attention off of Jesus and looked out at the storm around him, allowed his eyes and mind to wander to the fact that he was doing what no human should have been able to do. He let his logic take over and faltered, focusing on the circumstances rather than on his Lord's ability to wade through the waves and take him to safety. He let doubt cloud his perception and was quickly engulfed in waters from which he could not escape on his own. Yet while Peter was faithless, Jesus was faithful; He reached out without hesitation, lifting Peter out of the water despite his doubt.

Now faith doesn't require that we stop thinking; it calls us simply to meditate on the goodness and majesty of God. It asks that we see past our ordinary vision, past our best abilities, and further still to a God without limitations. We must trust, every moment, in a God that is all sufficient, all powerful, and more than able to lead. Minute by minute, step by step, onward and upwards.

08-19-2014

    This poem is less of a poem and more of a stream of consciousness. It's taken directly from a journal entry penned at a coffee shop on the date of its title. I remember sitting drinking my hot chocolate just overwhelmed by some of the things I felt God had been calling me to during that time. I remember being and feeling weighed down by the impossibility of my dreams and wanting to retreat. I recall reading this passage in Jeremiah and knowing it was for me, knowing that what God had spoken so many years ago was now being declared over me and that I needed to move forward believing in the promise.

    My prayer is that you'd be encouraged to move in the callings that God's placed on you. That you would dream big dreams and allow Him to use you to bring glory and honour to His name. That you would be a vessel, poured out in obedience to a master that is good and deserving of all the adoration and praise. I pray that wherever He calls you you'd have the faith to follow.

4 The word of the Lord came to me, saying,
5 "Before I formed you in the womb I knew you,
before you were born I set you apart;
I appointed you as a prophet to the nations."
6 "Alas, Sovereign Lord," I said, "I do not know how
to speak; I am too young."
7 But the Lord said to me, "Do not say, 'I am too
young.' You must go to everyone I send you to and
say whatever I command you.
8 Do not be afraid of them, for I am with you and will
rescue you," declares the Lord.
9 Then the Lord reached out his hand and touched
my mouth and said to me, "I have put my words in
your mouth.
(Jeremiah 1:4-9)

...Well I guess I feel like Jeremiah, wrestling with God
again and again over the truth of my identity. He's
told me to be brave. He's assured me that I'm fully
equipped with everything I could possibly need to
carry out His purposes. He knew me before He
formed me in the womb. I can't possibly make sense
of that. I was set apart before I was born. That is so,

so profound. Yet here I am, believing that despite His vast knowledge, His grandiose, infinite plan, He has somehow made a mistake and I am not the girl for the job. He's told me that He's with me; He's touched my mouth and given me His words. He's trusted me with His words. That's weighty... I feel too young. I don't believe that I'm capable. God really does delight in using the weak...

"Brothers and sisters, think of what you were when you were called. Not many of you were wise by human standards; not many were influential; not many were of noble birth. But God chose the foolish things of the world to shame the wise; God chose the weak things of the world to shame the strong." 1 Corinthians 1:27

"...But he said to me, "My grace is sufficient for you, for my power is made perfect in weakness." Therefore I will boast all the more gladly about my weaknesses, so that Christ's power may rest on me. That is why, for Christ's sake, I delight in weaknesses, in insults, in hardships, in persecutions, in difficulties. For when I am weak, then I am strong." 2 Corinthians 12:9-10

Doubt is uncomplicated. We don't have to learn how to do it. It doesn't take much to question, to challenge the things that we're told and rationalize our way towards apathy. When God brings things to our minds to do, gently nudging us as He often does, it becomes easy to disbelieve that we are capable of carrying them out. We reason that He must have made some sort of mistake, that if He really knew who He was dealing with He would never ask of us what He is. We are so sure that someone else is better for the job: someone smarter, older, braver, or more experienced. That if He only knew the full picture He would regret ever bringing the thing to our attention in the first place. I think when it comes to ourselves and our destinies, we are especially prone to retreat in fear and skepticism. We can feel paralyzed by the call, ignoring it entirely or pushing it off for some elusive start date. The issue when we do this is twofold; first in that it undermines God's wisdom, suggesting that we somehow know more about the situation, timing, or outcome than he does. Second, it communicates that He is not mighty enough to overcome our inadequacies, that His strength is somehow insufficient to make up for our shortcomings.

    The reality is, God will seldom call us to a task that is not wholly bigger than us. He does not spur us towards projects that we can accomplish in our own strength. God is keenly aware of our limitations, but also so confident in our potential through Him. He whisper to us "my grace is sufficient for you, for my power is made perfect in weakness." Feeling—even being—ill-equipped for a job is a beautiful thing. It teaches us to trust. It prepares us to learn to see beyond ourselves. It compels us to rely on God alone for help. Exercising faith means that we will necessarily go to places we are unsure of and compulsorily encounter situations we are not ready for. Following God doesn't require us to have it all together. We don't have to know everything or be particularly proficient. We can't be. There's not much you can do to prepare for a life of faith besides remind yourself continually that you can't possibly go it alone. At a certain point you must embrace the act of abandon, delight in the irony that the further you leap into the unknown, the more "experienced" you get, the more you understand that you don't understand. You, I, all of us, must grab hold of and even begin to glory in the fact that we are so in need of God and He is so prepared to come through for us. Let our hearts cry be like that of Paul's, boasting that "for Christ's sake, I delight in weaknesses, in insults, in hardships, in persecutions, in difficulties. For when I am weak, then I am strong."

Abundant

Looking back at this poem makes me feel like I'm reading my very own psalm. It's depressing. It's raw. It's a bit convoluted.

I find that too often I'm not entirely honest about where I'm at. I fail to admit when I lack faith and when believing gets hard. I rarely express when I have a difficult time believing in the promises I'm so quick to preach. The truth is, sometimes believing is difficult, and it's important to admit it. This piece is my unfiltered reflection on a period in my life when I failed to understand what God meant when He promised us abundant life. I didn't feel joyful, I couldn't see past the dullness of my circumstances. I felt dreary and uninspired and I found myself arguing with what I read and heard in light of what I was experiencing.

In the end however, I learnt that sometimes you have to choose joy, that it's not always something you feel but something you pursue believing in the promises of God as truth. I pray that joy becomes real to you regardless of your circumstances, that you receive a full, complete portion of the abundant life offered in Christ.

Exceedingly.
Abundantly.
Above all we could ask or think according to the power that works within us…
I was promised an abundant life. Not abundant in possessions or wealth or any of that noise but abundant in joy.
I was promised by a God who delivers on His word
So
I'm wondering why at times my life seems so painfully void.
I'm wondering how I'm supposed to show to the world that my God is worth living for if my life seems dead
I'm wondering how I'm to communicate that this race is worth walking out when my steps are lethargic at best
I can't live out the example of Christ if I don't exemplify the abundant life.
He promised.

He said in His presence is fullness of joy
And
I'd enjoy drinking up His cup 'til from fullness it runneth over
But
As of right now I'm running on about half empty
Steering down the road of my future searching for more than monotony
Yearning for something to stir me
Believe me.
I'd like to believe that abundant is possible
In the core of my being I want joy unstoppable
I want nothing to separate me from the love of God
I want a life so rich in Him I'd forsake treasures for my king
I want what's promised.
So
I'm going after it.
I want each moment of my life to be a testament.
Testifying
Of the God who poured out His life
So that I might live mine
Exceedingly.

Abundantly.
Above what I could dream.
I want the God who fulfills desires
Beyond what I can think.

"Now to Him who is able to do exceedingly abundantly above all that we ask or think, according to the power that works in us" Ephesians 3:20 (NKJV)

 Believing is difficult. I don't think that faith comes naturally to many of us. We are so intrinsically trained to trust with our five senses; if we can't tangibly perceive the things that go on around us we don't quite identify with them as truth. In speaking to the Ephesians, Paul prayed that they would be filled with the spirit's power such that they would be firmly established in the faith: "I pray that out of his glorious riches he may strengthen you with power through his Spirit in your inner being, so that Christ may dwell in your hearts through faith" (Ephesians 3:16-17). In this, Paul emphasizes the essential quality of God's involvement in our faith development. We are incredibly limited, and so susceptible to disbelieving

His promises. In our own strength we can't get there, we must ask God to take us to a place of genuine faith. At the same time, Paul demonstrated that Christ dwells in each of our hearts through faith, that aside from trusting in Him we cannot have Him reside within us. Philippians 2:12-13 puts it this way: "Therefore, my dear friends, as you have always obeyed—not only in my presence, but now much more in my absence—continue to work out your salvation with fear and trembling, for it is God who works in you to will and to act in order to fulfill his good purpose". In other words, God empowers us to believe Him as well as to walk out our belief. There is a power at work within us, the Holy Spirit, and it is He who enables us to trust God in every circumstance of our life. Whether well fed or in need, healthy or sick, we can do all things, through Christ who gives us strength. When faith gets hard, when believing feels a far cry from where you are, remember that you have a helper, remember that He is in you and that He is capable of immeasurably more than you can possibly ask for or imagine; lean in.

Esther 4:14

This poem came at a time of intense transition. I went from having a clear cut, secure vision of my future to diving head first into the unknown. I found myself so powerless, so limited in my understanding of my circumstances. God had begun to tear down so many of the things I'd for so long clung to for identity, (false) security, and comfort.

I learnt during this time that faith and familiarity can seldom co-exist, that if we don't leave room for God to move in our lives He can't. God can only be as big as we allow Him to be, when we erect idols and create for ourselves lives that require no dependence on Him, we limit the surpassing, abundant fulfillment that He's so graciously offered. I remember reading Esther and realizing that I needed to press into what God had planned for me in this new, unknown season. I saw myself as a servant not unlike her, commissioned for the present time to accomplish the purposes of God exactly where He had placed me. All I needed to do was trust Him. My prayer is that you would see God's hand directing and his voice calling and that you'd answer, fully aware that He's placed you for a purpose, entirely assured that He's with you wherever you go.

It's time.
Now begins my faith walk.
It's the first time I can actually say that I'm stepping into territory that's unknown,
And I don't know whether this thing I'm believing might blow up in smoke.
Feeling distant like the God I'm serving is less Holy and more Ghost
Uncertain about whether I can do this alone.
But—
It's time for faith.
It's time to seek His face cause if He doesn't come through there's not a thing I can do
So,
I'm trusting in His plan, and I may not understood but,
I've been told to lean not on my own understanding
So,
In Christ's word I am standing.

Trusting,
Believing,
That I've been commissioned,
"For such a time as this",
And I know the God I follow wouldn't tell me a myth…

"For if you remain silent at this time, relief and deliverance for the Jews will arise from another place, but you and your father's family will perish. And who knows but that you have come to your royal position for such a time as this?" Esther 4:14

"Trust in the LORD with all your heart
  and lean not on your own understanding;
in all your ways submit to him,
  and he will make your paths straight."
Proverbs 3:5-6

    When God calls us out, when He makes a vision clear to us and brings a part of our destiny to our attention, He does so with impeccable timing. In His sovereignty He is supreme over time, working always with full and complete knowledge of past, present, and future in a way that we aren't capable of comprehending.

Our lives have a funny way of overlapping with those of others, our fates converging in peculiar ways. When Esther came to her position, she couldn't have possibly grasped the enormity of what God had in store for her future. He had a plan to redeem the Jewish people, and as it was, she would be the one to see it through. Esther was promoted to her place of royalty from lowly beginnings. She was an ordinary Jewish girl who found favour in the eyes of a king and rose to great influence as a result. Beyond her earthly title, she had favour in God's eyes, and God had opened doors such that she would be an integral part of bringing justice and mercy for Jewish people across the land.

Overwhelmingly, Esther's greatest strength was her obedience to the call of God. Faith in God commissioned her to act on behalf of her people, even with the threat of death. She demonstrated faith in action, standing up on behalf of those in need. She must have understand what Paul talks about when he asks, "What good is it, my brothers and sisters, if someone claims to have faith but has no deeds?"; she must have understood that "faith by itself, if it is not accompanied by action, is dead" (James 2:14-17). Once called she moved forth in confidence, displaying her faith and prepared to face death if necessary. She was empowered with the knowledge that God had called her for a specific purpose and despite the odds, He would be faithful to come through. Esther possessed an assuredness in the role she was in, not because she thought herself particularly proficient for the task but because she knew her God was. 1 Corinthians 1:28 says that "God chose the lowly things of this world and the despised things—and the things that are not—to nullify the things that are." See God calls us wherever we are, in spite of ourselves and uses us to accomplish His incredible redemptive plans. We have the honour of saying yes, of allowing Him to use us exactly where and when He intends to. The question is not will He call us, but rather, will we answer the call.

{ Transfixed }

This poem is about straining to keep my eyes on God in the midst of so many distractions. We've been called the most distracted generation and I believe it. From social media to the entertainment industry to the constant bombardment of advertising we are so apt to get lost in things that ultimately do not matter. I find that I desire to keep God first but there is still so much within me that fights for His affection. I'm prone to wander, predisposed to erect idols in His place and believe lies instead of truth. My heart fails to trust that He is the ultimate source of satisfaction. I'm conditioned to doubt that He's good and that all I will ever need is Him. Under pressure I forsake and reject Him. In good times I forget that I need Him.

This poem confronts all this. This poem is a battle cry to my heart, mind, and soul to return to a life of full allegiance to Him. This poem is a call to once and for all leave idols at the altar and take up the cross. I pray that in reading it you'd find your heart in a place of full surrender, ready to trust Him, poised to follow.

8 I have set the Lord always before me;
  because he is at my right hand, I shall not be shaken.
9 Therefore my heart is glad, and my whole being rejoices;
  my flesh also dwells secure.
10 For you will not abandon my soul to Sheol,
  or let your holy one see corruption.
11 You make known to me the path of life;
  in your presence there is fullness of joy;
  at your right hand are pleasures forevermore.
(Psalm 16: 8-11)

...Fighting to fix my eyes on the very source of light
That is I'm
Aiming to remain seeking it out til the day that I die
Fighting to follow all the days of my life
Straining to stay transfixed
I—
Run to distractions like they're my alibi
Focused in as the apple of my eye
I water down and compromise
Overlook Adonai

And I know that I am prone to forsake the truth for worldly lies
Where the wind blows I'm tempted to go
When the tide flows I head for the shore
Directionless don't know south from the north
But
He makes known to me the path of life
In His presence is fullness of joy
At His right pleasures forevermore
So
I can't look to what was left anymore
Can't return to the places I've been delivered out of
I will
Fight to remain
Strain to seek His face
I'll fix my eyes incessantly
On the finisher of my faith
For
What is seen is temporary
The unseen eternal
Would I see through lenses transcendent
Beyond today and tomorrow
So would my gaze remain

On the Ancient of Days
Transfixed
Towards heaven
Always.

"But whatever were gains to me I now consider loss for the sake of Christ. What is more, I consider everything a loss because of the surpassing worth of knowing Christ Jesus my Lord, for whose sake I have lost all things. I consider them garbage, that I may gain Christ and be found in him, not having a righteousness of my own that comes from the law, but that which is through faith in Christ."
Philippians 3:8-9

"So we fix our eyes not on what is seen, but on what is unseen, since what is seen is temporary, but what is unseen is eternal." 2 Corinthians 4:18

When Jesus commissioned the twelve disciples He did so with a simple plea: "Follow me". It wasn't a complicated call to get themselves together or prepare or train or plan an elaborate journey, but just to walk with Him wherever He went. For the next three years, wherever Jesus was they were. They journeyed alongside Him as He healed the sick, comforted the broken, cared for the forgotten, died and rose, and eventually ascended into Heaven. They lived life together, keenly intent to follow in His footsteps and see the world radically changed.

More than 2000 years later, we get to do the same. We too can go where Jesus went and love and serve as He did. The life of faith is one of following. It's a matter of walking in the footsteps of those that came before us. In Hebrews 11, we see a record of many of the pioneers of faith, individuals who followed God regardless of the costs. Many of them died never seeing the complete fruit of their labour, they weren't praised by the people around them or esteemed to places of power. They were simply devoted followers, infatuated by a good king, and determined to press on in their lives of faith. Entranced by the prospect of better days, verse 16 explains that they were longing for a "better country", a Heavenly one. They were so focused on God, on the life to come, that they considered all else a massive loss in comparison to knowing and being known by Jesus. Each of them clung to the vision of God as central. They simply ran the race of their faith, intent to finish strong. In Hebrews 12:2, Paul summarizes the journey of faith as a "looking unto Jesus", a setting one's sights on "the author and finisher of faith, who for the joy that was set before Him endured the cross." It's a matter of continuing to look to Christ, of catching a glimpse of Him and resolving to spend the rest of your life seeking Him out—fix your eyes; keep the pace; finish the race.

"Therefore, since we are surrounded by such a huge crowd of witnesses to the life of faith, let us strip off every weight that slows us down, especially the sin that so easily trips us up. And let us run with endurance the race God has set before us."
Hebrews 12:1 (NLT)

IN CLOSING

If you've made it this far I'd like to thank you. Thanks for allowing me to share my heart with you. Thanks for listening. Thanks for being a part of the journey.

I pray that you'd be encouraged by something you read here. I pray you'd move forward with deeper revelations of truth and that you'd carry them with you everywhere you go.

Know that you are dearly loved by God and that the life He offers is the best one possible. Be free in the reality of who He's made you to be and in the beauty of your purpose.

Would you be both blessed and a blessing. Keep learning; keep growing; keep loving.

Sincerely,

Deb

"And we all, who with unveiled faces contemplate the Lord's glory, are being transformed into his image with ever-increasing glory, which comes from the Lord, who is the Spirit."

2 Corinthians 3:18

Made in the USA
Charleston, SC
09 September 2015